Dance Against the Wind

By Mir Foote

©2012 by MIR Foote

All photographs within are the property of Mir Foote with the exception of 'See' (pg 36) which was included with permission from the owner.

All rights reserved.

ISBN-13: 978-1470108878
ISBN-10: 1470108879

For my mom, my dad, my grandparents, and everyone who ever encouraged me to write.

Table of Contents

Forward	7
Dance of Birds	9
Drums	11
The Light Bulb	12
Roses	17
Beyond	18
June Bug	19
Forest Pine	21
Is the Universe a Ship?	23
Drum	25
Light	26
On a Night	27
The Carpenter	28
An Autumn Poem	31
The Bench	33
See	34
Mistress of Mercy	39
The Pied Piper	40
Babylon	43
Wind	44
Winter	45
Seashore	47
Asphalt Heaven	48
Ice Age	49
Fey	51
Rocking Chair Wings	53
Strangers	54
Dance Against the Wind	57
About the Author	60

Forward

If there is one activity in this world that I love, it is to make words dance. They have been my playground for as far back as my memory can stretch. In the beginning, before I could write, I lived in my stories. Everything had a story. I could sit perfectly contented with a box of pencils while I dreamed up personalities and backgrounds for each one. Math class, for me, was a continuous numeric war wherein 7 was meek, 8 quite vicious and evil, and 9 far too lordly. And of course, I learned at last to write my stories down.

Everyone told me I should be a writer. So I wrote. Looking back at my earliest work, I must admit I was not that particularly gifted. I was imaginative, definitely, but I was young and I wrote like the child I was. But I kept writing, because I was encouraged. I was encouraged by my parents and teachers. I was encouraged by the librarians who ran programs at the Emily Fowler Public Library. I was encouraged by the universal dance group my father took me to on Fry Street. I never stopped writing.

Eventually, I began to win awards for my poetry. At school, at the library, 1st place ribbons and trophies started to appear. Now I've had about twenty years of experience writing, and continue to win awards, my latest being 1st place with the NCTC 2011 Regional Poetry Contest with my poem 'Dance of Birds'.

For this book, I have selected the best of my poetry written in the later years. They are my playground, my journey, my dreams, and my soul. Whether you find in them wells of wisdom or trivial delights of speech, I hope you enjoy the dance.

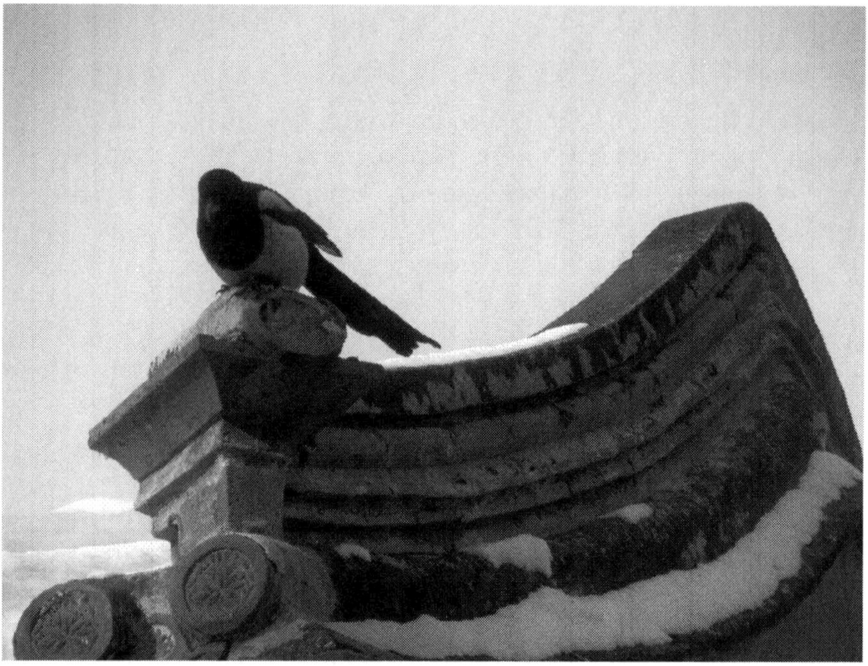

Dance of Birds

In ruffled dress of brightest hue,
or silvered gowns of white and gray,
in styled suit of earthy brown,
or solemn black, all greet the day.

The sunlight wakes the morning ball,
and sharply breaks across a floor
bedecked in dew like silver stars
left over from the night before.

The dancers come, in threes and fours,
bow to the wind in flurried flight,
joining once more on feathered wing,
walk out upon the rays of light.

The choir erupts among the leaves;
the sky has turned from black to gold;
the music thrills upon the wind,
the oldest language ever told.

And how the dancers leap and sway!
Now bold, now shy, now high aloft,
as throats give voice to first of day,
piercing and sharp and sweet and soft.

And all of life awakes once more,
in that song devoid of words,
primal praise to dark's defeat,
within the dawn of dancing birds.

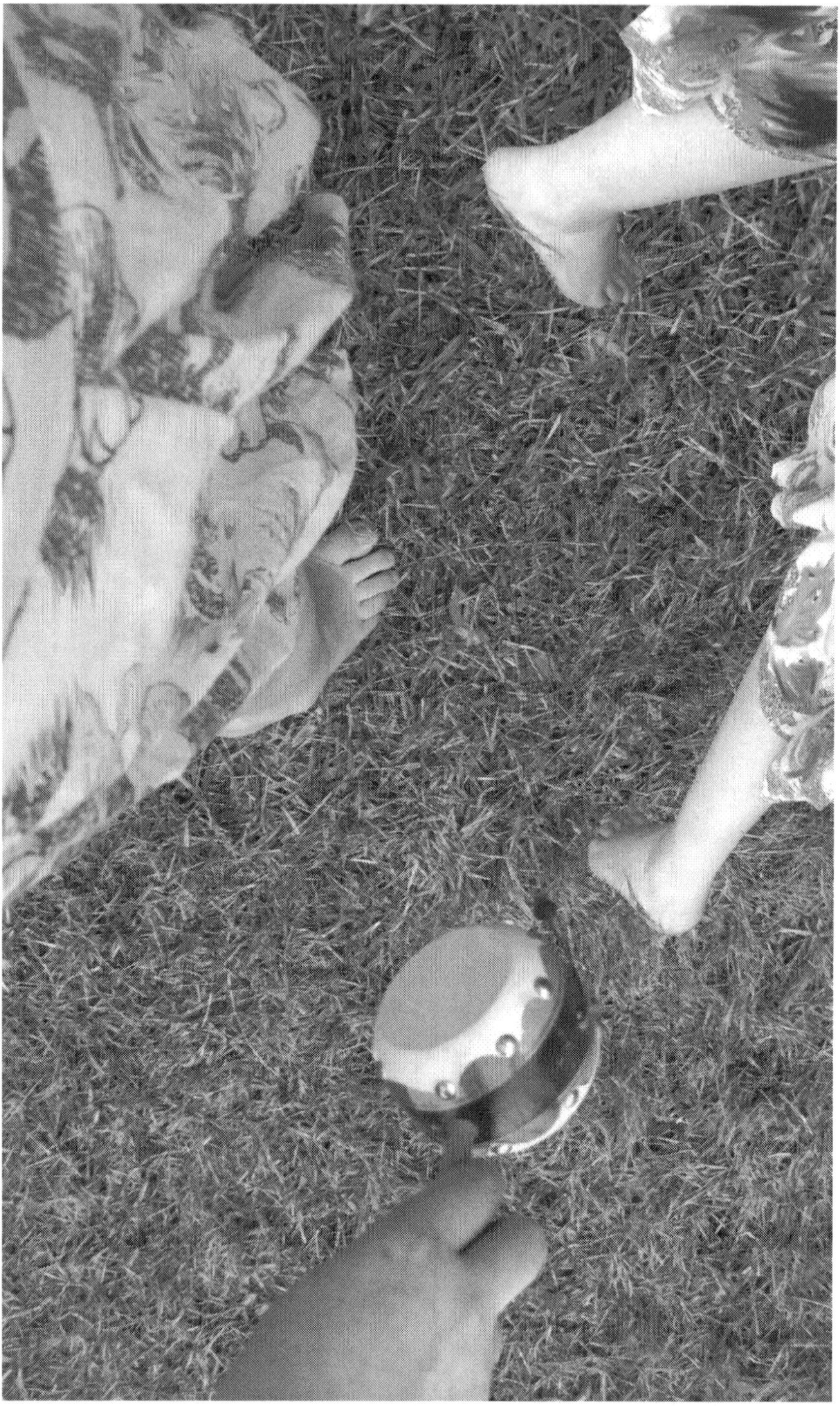

Drums

Bare feet stamp the earth
dancing to the rhythm
of ancient drums.

The fire leaps high
all the way to the moon
and burns holes in the darkness.

Ancient spirits swim the waters
looking back on the cold
before life and dance
and sweep about the ashes.

They lift their voices high and free
defiant to the empty dark:

Here am I
Now
Now
Now
I am

There they rise and there they fall
leaping flames in shadowed night.

And now
Now
Now
I am
And I dance
Dance
Dance

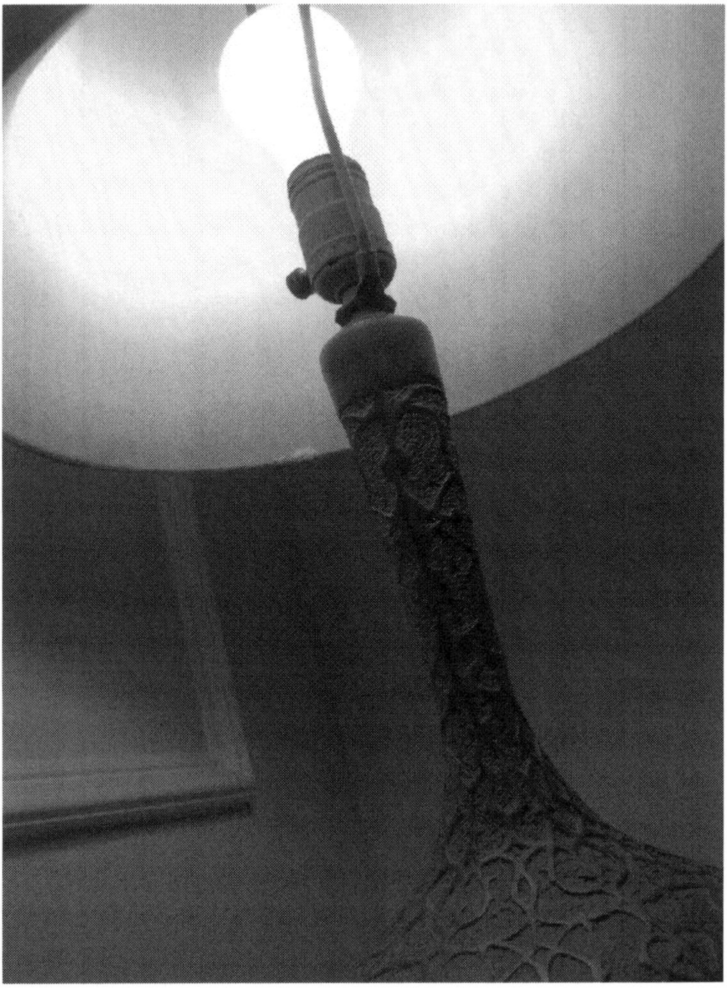

The Light Bulb

Childhood is always a time
caught between two worlds;
between dresses and grass stains,
between dragons and bedtimes,
sitting, legs crossed, as straight as an arrow,
and trying to stand on your head.
And sometimes one side wins;
when you remember your pleases
and thank you's,
to cover your mouth
when you sneeze.
But there are always those moments
when something must break out,
and one world collides with the other
so that anything can happen.
There was a party,
of a sorts,
in which many great aunts
and ancient family friends
gathered around in the evening,
as the great lords and ladies must have
in the olden times,
and I was permitted to stay up
in the background of their talk.
I was sitting idly in my chair
as the great lords and ladies around me droned on
with so many meaningless words,
growing quite drowsy,
and as they spoke,
carefully holding their cups,
I looked up and saw
on the table a lamp
trying its best to light the room,
but it was dim and flickered
just like a little firefly
caught in a jar.

I dreamed of millions of fireflies
let loose all at once from a Summer's Night
into the room
as I dosed in my chair
until my mother nudged me
to sit up straight
and some great Aunt discussed her birds
that were long dead,
and I stared at the flickering light
trying so hard to do its job,
as I slid back in my chair again
when suddenly it struck me,
clear as day:
it was no light bulb flickering there,
but a captured being of light
trying to escape the globe!
I saw it flit about
like Tinker Bell in Peter Pan,
now bursting forth in brilliant light,
now falling back, almost dead,
and my uncle, I think he was,
talked about a party long past,
amid polite laughter,
while the light became quite desperate,
and each flicker was less intense,
like a star fading in the dawn,
or the moon hiding behind the clouds.
And I just knew that all the world would end
should it go out.
And a friend of my mom's
rose up to refill his cup,
and the light made one last attempt
flaring bright and brilliant,
but I could not let it die,
ancient and withered into nothingness.
I leapt from my chair,

reaching out to save it,
knocking the lamp in my haste,
so that all leapt from the table
in a glorious dive,
and the globe burst into a million pieces,
with the lamp.
And I cried,
"Look, look, the light is free!"
And the light fled away
to wherever lights go,
to Neverland or Summer Nights
all rolled into one,
and I wanted to leap for joy,
but all they could see
was the broken glass upon the floor
and completely missed its flight.

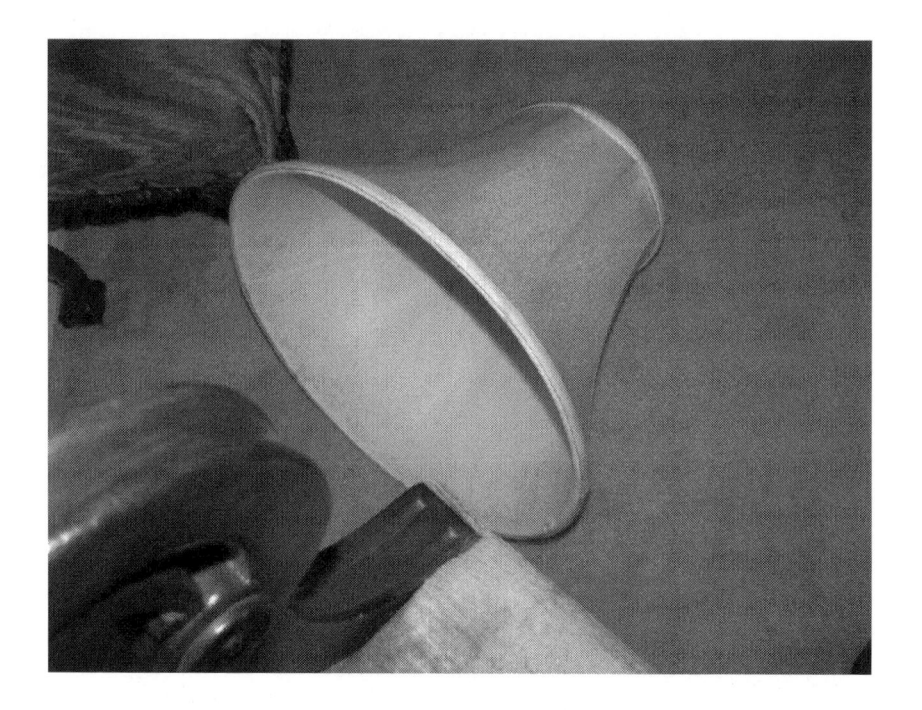

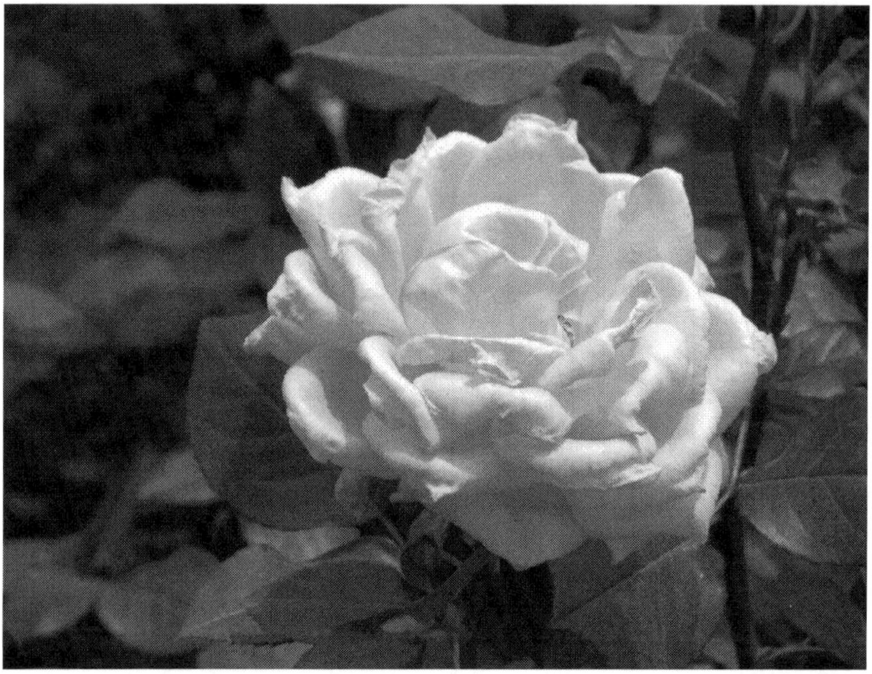

Roses

If I live until tomorrow,
a year older I will be,
but if I should die today,
tomorrow will never know me.

If I plant a hundred roses,
and all but one of them die,
is it the same as planting but one,
and never the ninety-nine?

And yesterday the roses were not,
and tomorrow they are no more;
if only today do the roses bloom,
then what are the roses for?

And in a hundred million years,
when all the roses are gone,
does it matter that my rose lived,
and who will remember its fall?

Beyond

    Beyond these walls a fair day calls,
    a joyous afternoon;
    the wind does play in the trees today,
    whistling a merry tune.
    The grass is soft and high aloft,
    the billowing clouds float by;
    the Church bells ring the birds all sing,
    beneath a clear blue sky.
    Beyond this room the flowers bloom,
    a sweet scent on the air;
    beneath the sun the children run,
    without a single care.
    Beyond this glass are hills of grass,
    a glorious day of spring,
    but in a chair from the desk I stare,
    and must miss the entire thing!

June Bug

You cannot take but what you bring,
you cannot see but what you've seen,
and so we look with blind, blind wing,
flying swift against the room,
'til falling to the dusty gloom,
so to fail the suns of June.

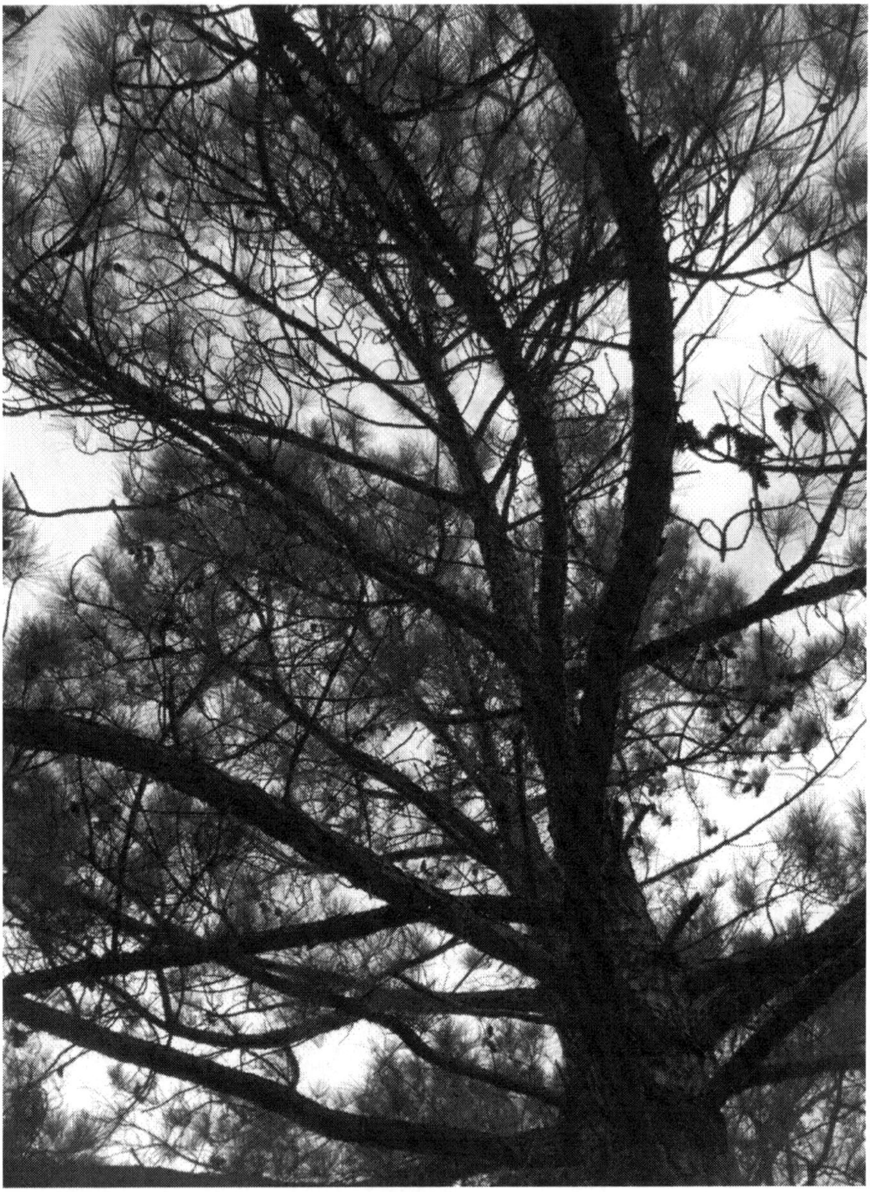

Forest Pine

The twisted wood of withered dark and gloom
of trees that reach into the forest night
are lost in ancient thoughts devoid of sight
where whispered sighs and memories consume.

Too dense for dreams these wizened giants loom,
listening for mortal tread beneath their height
and should one dare to stand in candle light
the crowding shadows hiss impending doom.

But soft the moonlight falls upon the pines
and shadows break upon the forest floor
and in the golden halls of ancient mines
their arching roots drink deep from Terra's core.

They hold for us as living, graven signs,
a witness to a world that came before.

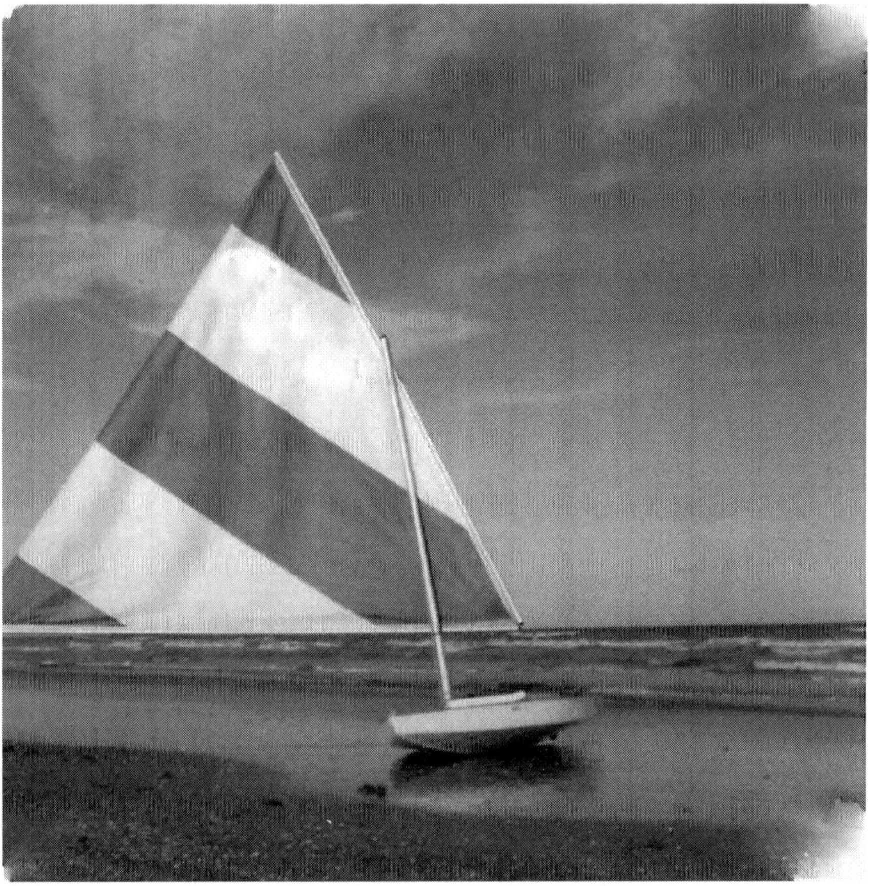

Is the Universe a Ship?

Is the universe a ship?
Or is it a waiting room,
or is it nothing at all and we only thought it was?
And if I lost my name,
and the depths of my eyes,
and I lay down beneath the water,
and found no light,
would I cease to be?
And if I am not,
then why am I here,
and if a person comes to you,
and speaks in Chinese,
and you say, "I am sorry, I do not speak Chinese"
can you still say that words have meaning?
And if they do not,
then I might scream beneath these waves,
waiting in the dark;
I will shout "Ship, ship!"
when I meant to say 'help'
I meant to say 'remember me'
when I meant to say a question, something profound,
but I couldn't find the words,
and the Chinese sailors might stop,
or they might sail on,
or they might never have been there at all,
and if they were not,
and I was not,
then perhaps we are not really here,
there is no here at all,
we only thought there was.

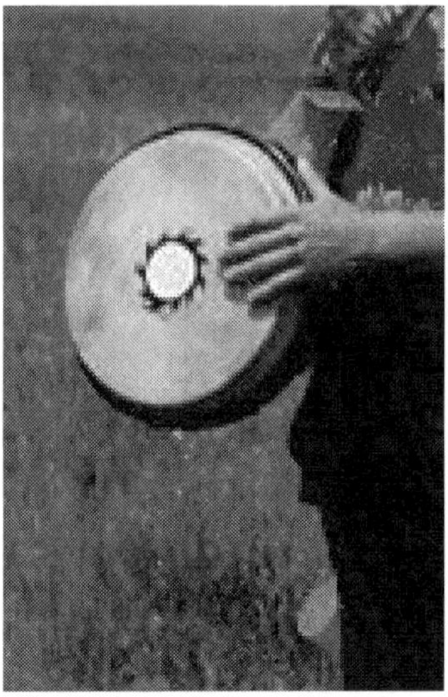

Drum

I dance in the world
to the beat of drums
and everything comes
in the spiraling spin
and the stomping feet
within the beat
to the silent end.

~

A howling cry
and the world defy
all beauty and pain
and the falling rain
the earth is strong
and the fire burns
and leaps to the night
of the earth
I dance
and leap with the stars
I see
the wild stars
and trailing light
that fades to dawn
and all the sleeping world
awakes and begins anew.

Light

Rage in the face of the dark and soulless light;
the honeyed voice of reason that slithers past the fight;
the fork tongued politician and the selfish right,
who gently gently leave our wings but steal the winds of flight.

_____On a Night

On a night,
an empty clear night,
alight with stars,
stand upon this Earth,
and look up,
and up,
and up,
until you must cling tight to the grass,
or fall.

The Carpenter

    My father's hands, rough and brown with weathered use,
    long, plyful fingers bent about their work,
    a carpenter, he shapes wood into dreams,
    searching over sketched blue print maps that shall become,
    a bench, a table, a house.

    Now he is making boxes,
    small, weather warped works,
    scenting of ancient pines:
    tall, sharp, strong,
    proud guardians to an older world.

Here now they lie,
the scattered scraps of colder, lesser frames -
the last remains falling from
a set of drawers, a desk, a door.

And so he takes this salvaged wood,
and finds four sides upon a sturdy base,
wild wooden walls-
not perfect smooth tamed wood,
carefully harvested, all holes filled,
every indention and character sawed away.

No, he leaves them as found,
only sanding them to shape-
four climbing sides upon one root,
and last the crown is placed, a lid, loosely square,
to hold all the emptiness within.

"Why do you make these boxes,"
someone asked him once,
"of these rough left over scraps?"
And he answered:
"This wood was once a tree.
Now I make its coffin."

He takes these empty boxes,
and sells them,
to be filled as they will,
with sweet scented forest memories,
ancient, whispered, forgotten attic dreams.

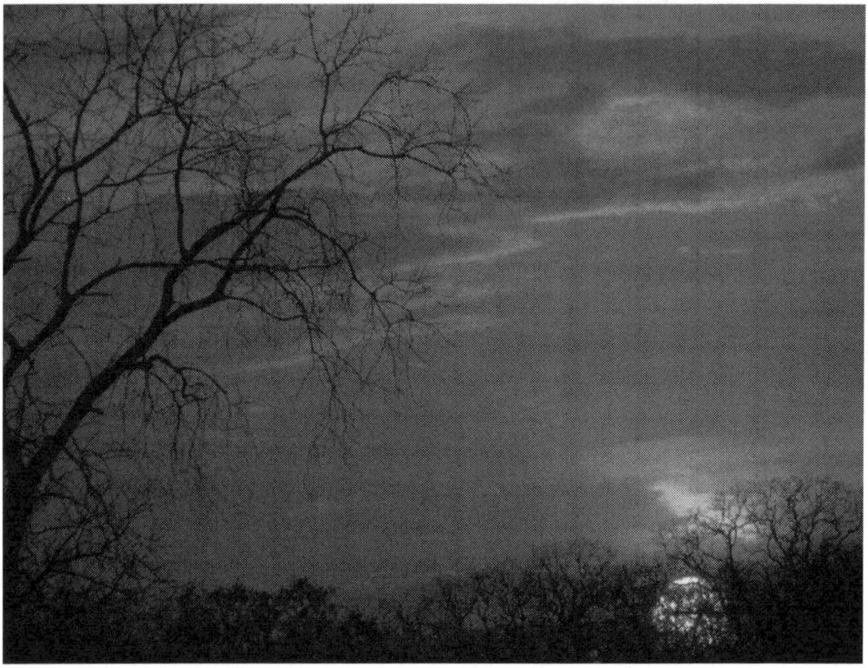

An Autumn Poem

Beauteous! Oh most beautiful of Death I see,
grasping tight to twisted aging tree:

forgotten green of old this curled, dry worn Spring,
release these golden death to dance on wing!

Alighting soft at last on hallowed ground,
cracked and carven stone where lost is found,

and though the gold is raked and swept away,
scattered over with flowers for a day,

and old remembered green and life that was before,
until there's no one left to rake the floor,

but still the golden withered death must fall,
over pillared stones of gray shall cover all.

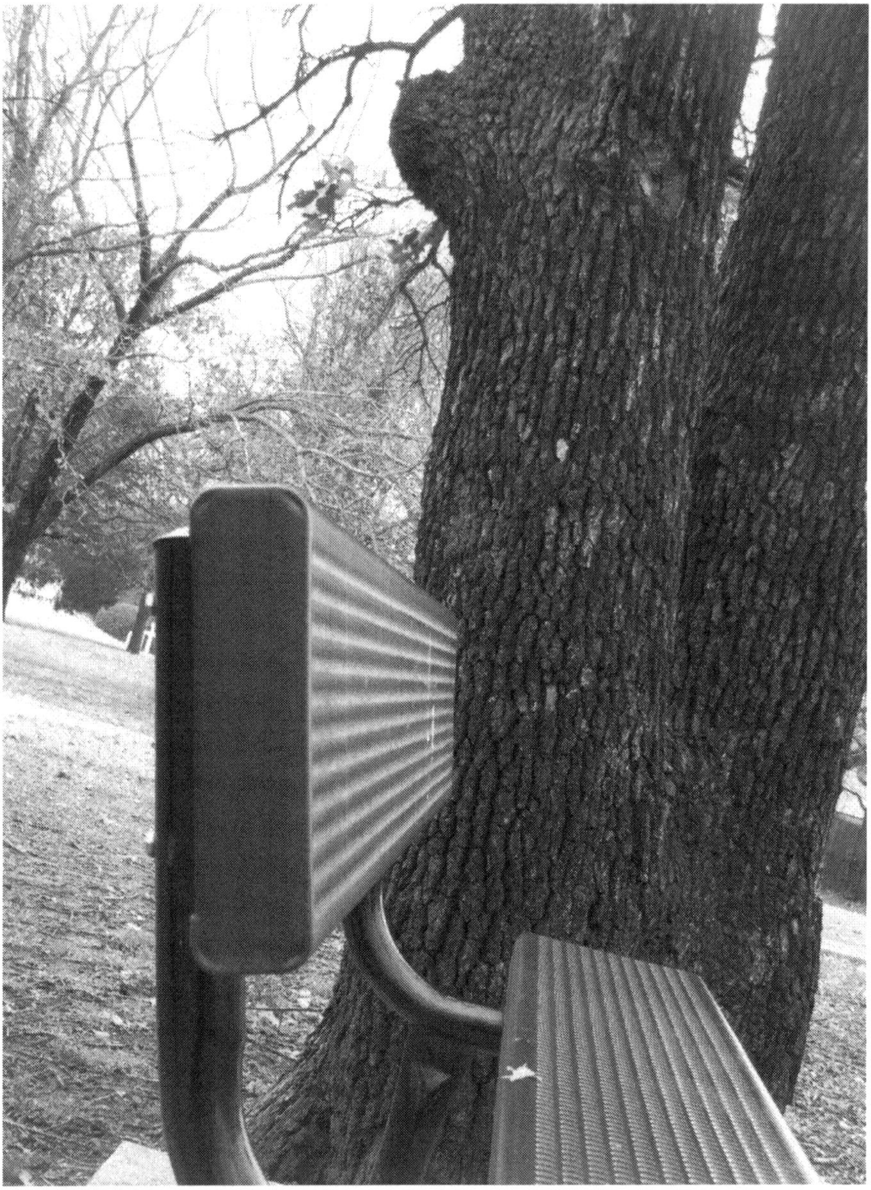

The Bench

Within a park I saw a bench,
beneath a great tall tree;
the wind that day was cold and chill,
and no one was there but me.

The withered tree was brown and bare,
the sky forlorn and gray,
and all alone the bench sat there,
waiting, for a warmer day.

Around me tight I grasped my coat;
I meant to hurry on,
then I heard the branches moan,
a sigh of springs long gone.

I stood a moment against the wind,
then came beneath that tree,
and all together we sat alone,
the bench the tree and me.

See _____

It begins
> you must open your eyes,
> and you will begin to see;
> don't bar these windows to your soul,
> but let them run glistening free.
> Take in now a breath of air,
> breathe in   The wide free sky,
> throw out your arms as the wind sweeps past,
> a whispered, musical sigh;

tell now a story completely absurd,
dance on Pinocchio's nose,
insist that two and two equals five,
stop to taste a rose.
Leap into the water clear,
as the rain falls on your head,
now is the time to laugh and live,
'til the stars are ancient and dead,
and when the world falls and when the earth breaks,
and rain turns to acid and fills up the lakes,
and the stars fade away and the sky burns with fumes,
the Earth paved in concrete and not one rose blooms,
they give you a sword and adventure and power,
the story unfolds in the space of an hour,
there grand before you larger than life,
and there's pain and there's joy and hunger and strife,
and you feel in you strength of all of the world,
and it burns and it rips and it bites,
and blood runs free and your eyes turn to ice,
and your soul is trapped inside.
Wade then through your filth,
you're standing on bones,
and blood burns as acid this Earth,
and it is too too much to hold to hold,
and throw out your hands as wide,
as you can,
but the world is larger than you.
And there's Death.
It ends.
That's it, don't you see?
You must see that it ends,
now open your eyes,
and there's death, things die,
crumble and fall,
and you will be gone,
your body must break,
and shrivel and rot in the earth,
And you.
What will there be after death?

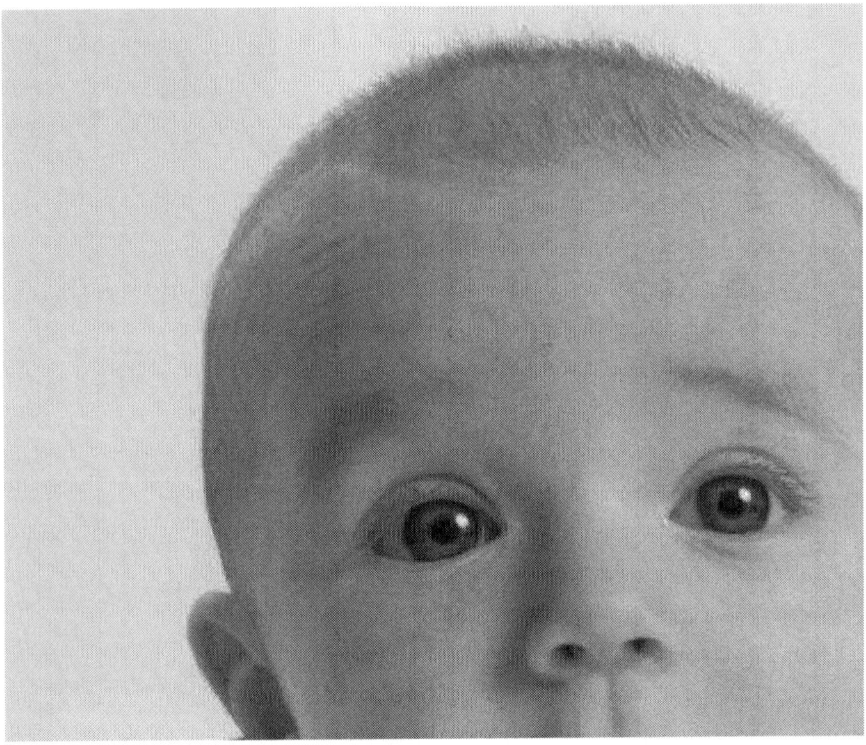

How does it end?
The dark and cold empty alone,
everything gone and changed.
And when you see, truly see,
that you must die,
you were born to die,
everything moves ever to its end,
see this,
know this,
and now,
now,
NOW
OPEN YOUR EYES.

And the sun is shining,
a world full of strangers,
blind men and beggars and poets and kings,
and there are flowers still, and stars, and such things;
there are books filled with whispers of people long gone,
and everywhere new things, beginnings and song,
and out in the sky are worlds never seen,
endless, unending the sky;
take up again your happy thought,
and remember how to fly.
And why is it that you are as you are?
And life!
We exist,
we are, don't you see,
and you are as you are,
and I will be me;
face all the questions of the world,
its pain and its beauty and life,
see all the colors and hear all the sound,
know this and see,
look beyond the beginning,
beyond the end,
open your eyes,
and see.

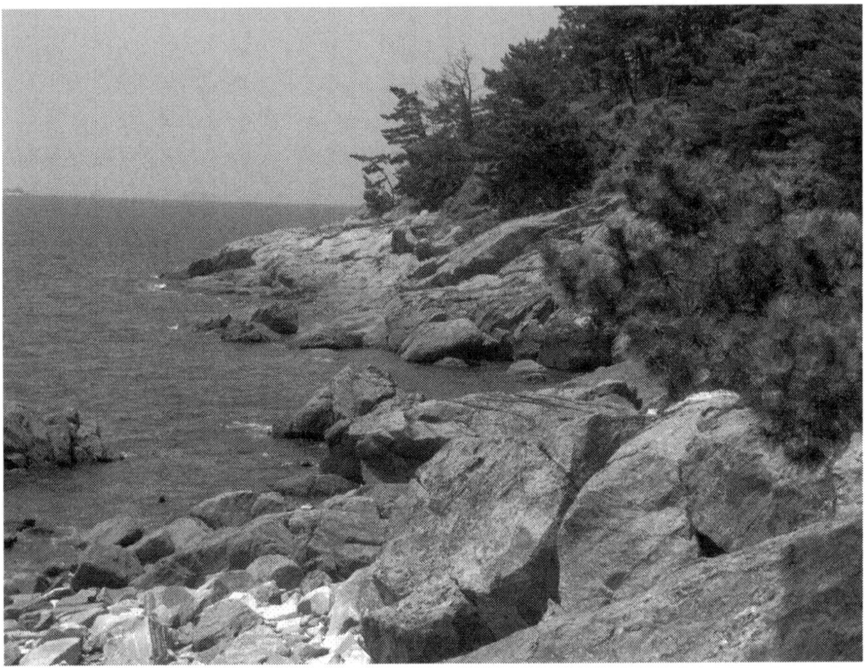

Mistress of Mercy

Mistress of Time,
I'll give thee a dime,
if thou'lt give a century for me,
'til pain is grown old,
and memories cold,
lost to the tumbling sea.

To live a full minute,
with eons within it,
and the heartache of Now's faraway,
'til all left beholden,
are memories golden,
and all that is pain's flown away.

The Pied Piper

There was a land of many peoples,
they got along fair well,
everyone within their world-
the Pied Piper cast his spell.

This music begged no questions.
it told such coaxing tales.
we must away with rats it cried.
all difference repels.

These Others they are not like Us,
we are Right and they are Wrong,
dangerous or unholy ones,
so now come gather to the song.

    It whispers what all need to know,

it plays on hidden hopes and fears,
it creeps into those deepest hearts-
everything is clear.

And will some refuse the luring tune?
Standing alone, closed ears, aloof,
screaming deaf upon deaf ears,
but no one is completely piper proof.

And are you the rat who will not hear,
or are you now a harmless mouse,
lost to words of righteousness,
hidden trembling within our house?

So follow follow the piper's song,
dance away wherever it leads,
into the river and evil is drowned!
On righteous spirit the music feeds.

But know you not the piper's cost,
will not you pay the piper's song?
Away with the children dance beyond,
to the music they belong.

Take the strong and leave the weak,
lost within the music wrung,
the piper's song just must be paid;
buy salvation with our young.

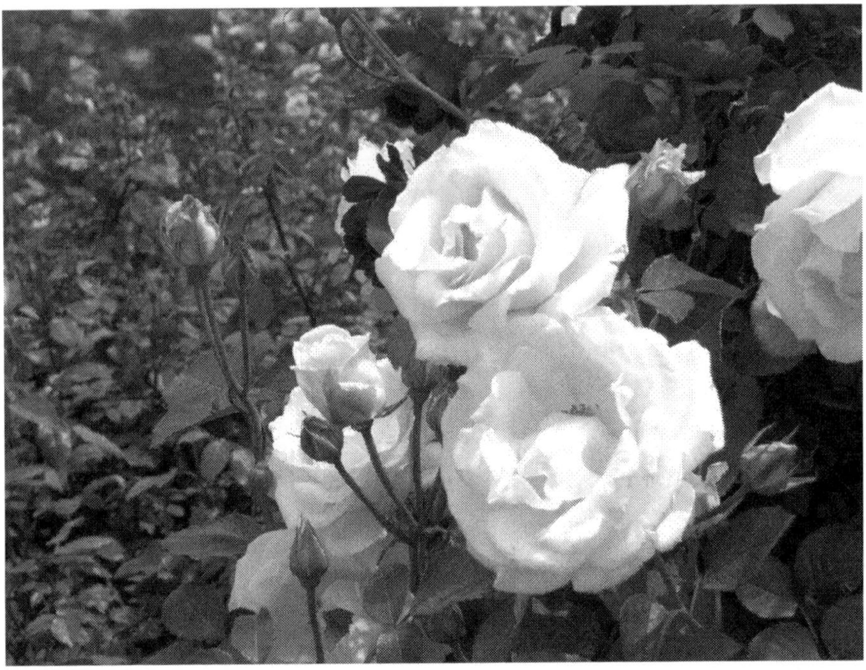

Babylon

My Grandmother sits upon her porch, surrounded by the sweet flowers of the past, children long grown, dogs, birds, planted deep into the moist rich earth. She knew an entire garden once, whispered to each their secret names, raised them by her own hand, fulfilling her garden. Roses climb up the porch, building bridges above our heads where birds meet. Geese run hissing through tall grasses where wilderness runs into plowed lines of beans. Carrots hide beneath the earth among daffodils and the wild bush blossoms purple as it reaches over the path. Here she prunes, there she feeds, each to its own need. Like the sunflower seeking light she follows the sweet blossom's scent over a lifetime of flowers.

Now, she fills her eyes with seeds, digs deeper her roots and sprouts fruit from her lips. Through her eyes there comes the light of the sun, filling the air with green fountains. Far beyond the broken gate, out beyond the mailboxes, over the fields, upon the wings of birds, of butterflies, the laughter of the wind. She builds and shapes and grows in green whispers, remembering and enveloping until her garden becomes a field of stars. Encircling the skies with red and yellow and orange, beckoning to bees and fluttering leaves, still her flowers bloom.

Wind

Wind whispers wintering way,
wild and howling the deepening night,
weeping ice in the blue shattered day,
laughing the vast wild flight.

Into eternity, scream to be free,
broken the circle, beginning and end,
crumbled destruction, lost all that be,
remembers the free howling wind.

Winter

The bitter cold strikes
with spears of ice,
a wind of force that rips
the leaves from trees
and turns the world to white,
but I will not hide,
huddled in my cave,
hands and face turned black
in the shadows of my flame;
I shall run out laughing;
I shall ride the howling winds,
and face the empty ice,
breath of smoke and burning ears,
singing in the silence of the world.
Never will I cling to my leaves;
withered death I throw you to the wind!
I walk the cold dead earth,
laughing blue and white
beneath the glittering skies,
a thousand jewels of ice;
I leap into the ocean white
to outdance the cold,
creating there an angel where I fall.

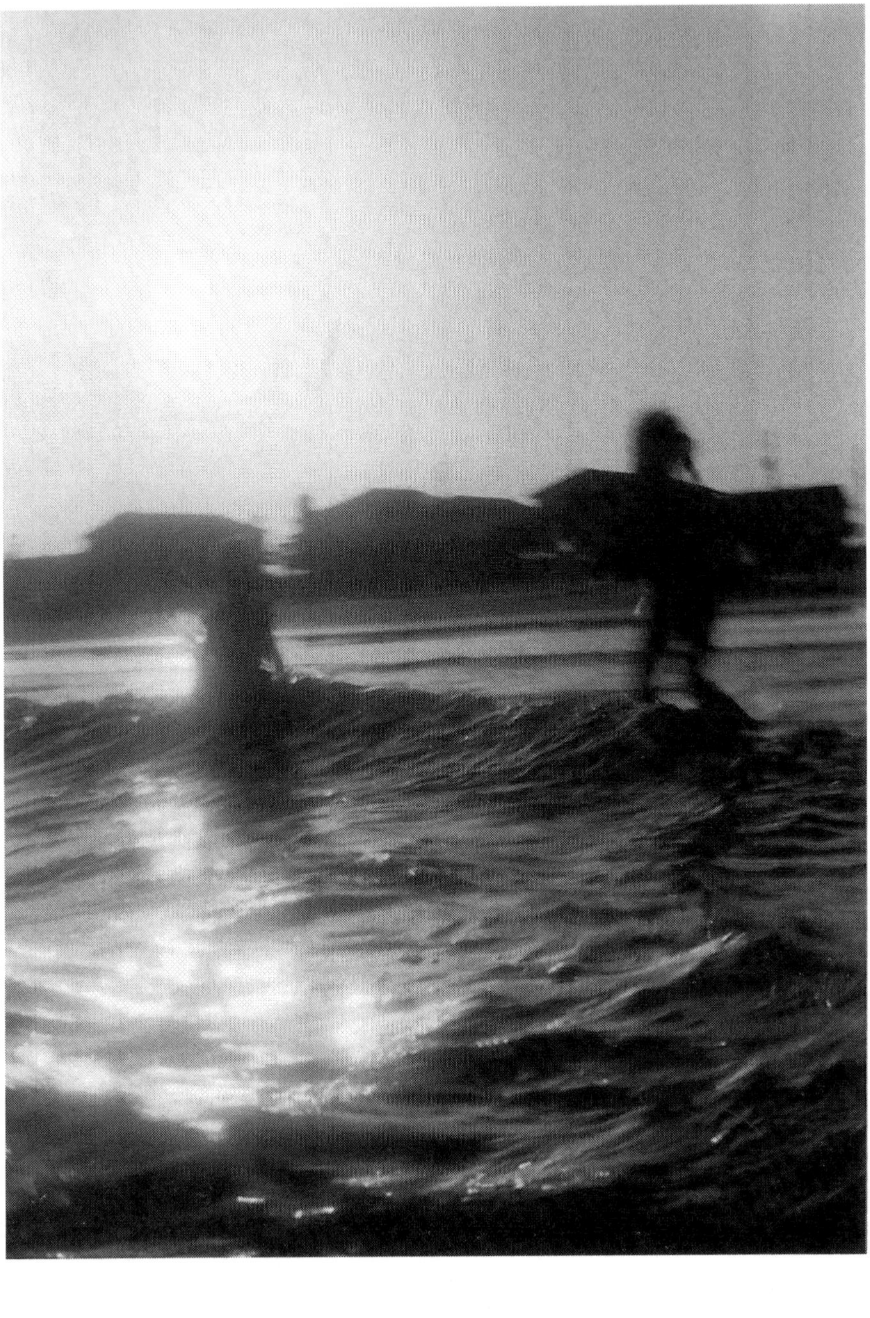

Seashore

Deep within the ocean's foam,
the sun folds into fractured worlds,
broken light in prison white,
whispered gleam in murky home.

The sand is wet and thirsts for feet,
digging for treasured tooth and shell,
gifts that hide where sparkles glide,
in dance where sands and waters meet.

There between two offered worlds,
the sun meets wave and wave licks shore,
footsteps fill with sea's fierce will,
'til wave takes back what feet have bored.

In brilliance of the setting sun,
ocean mingles with distant sky,
horizons meet for moments fleet,
and shadows blend 'til all is one.

Asphalt Heaven

Pebbled crystals shatter light,
scattering stars beneath my feet:
a hidden asphalt Milky Way,
and more of the universe might be seen
in this deserted night paved field
than all the glowing smog warmed skies.

Ice Age

When all the world is ice and snow,
and we may play at Eskimo,
and look back upon our future times,
and promises for hotter climes,
and forward see our ancient past,
then we shall know what is to last.

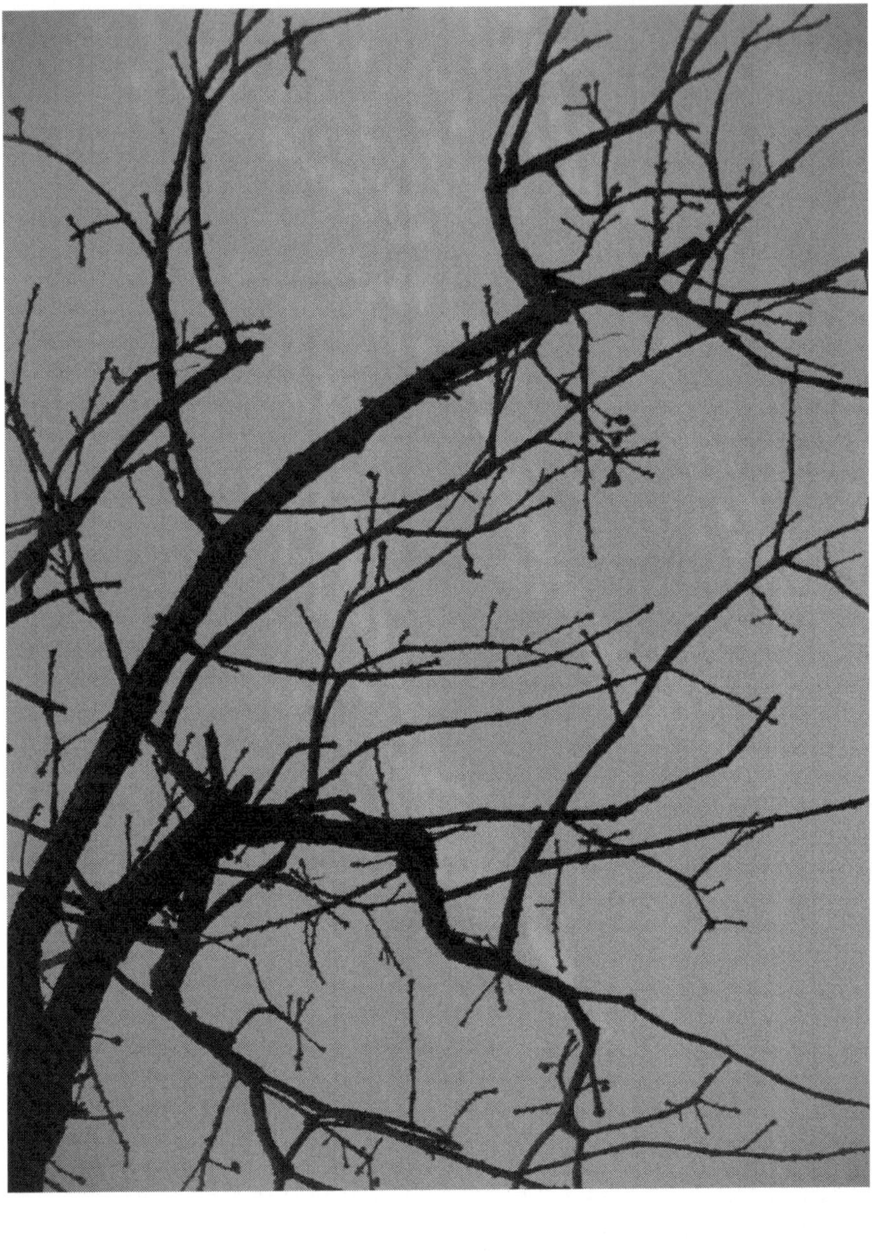

Fey

Walking silent into the night,
I stand upon a leafless path;
in shadowed flame of lantern light,
I see the mournful moths flit past.

The sky is veiled in blackest gray;
no stars, nor moon shall find me here,
not but the phantom lights of fey,
dance from some long forgotten fear.

I am alone and not alone;
the wind is warm like whispered breath;
I hear a tune of wild tone,
sweet and sorrowful as death.

Between the shadows shifting stare,
twigs reach out devoid of sight
to grasp at passing ropes of hair
and cast their bones to startled flight.

I stare into the starless sky,
between the skeletons of trees,
and wonder at how small am I,
alone and fleeting as the breeze.

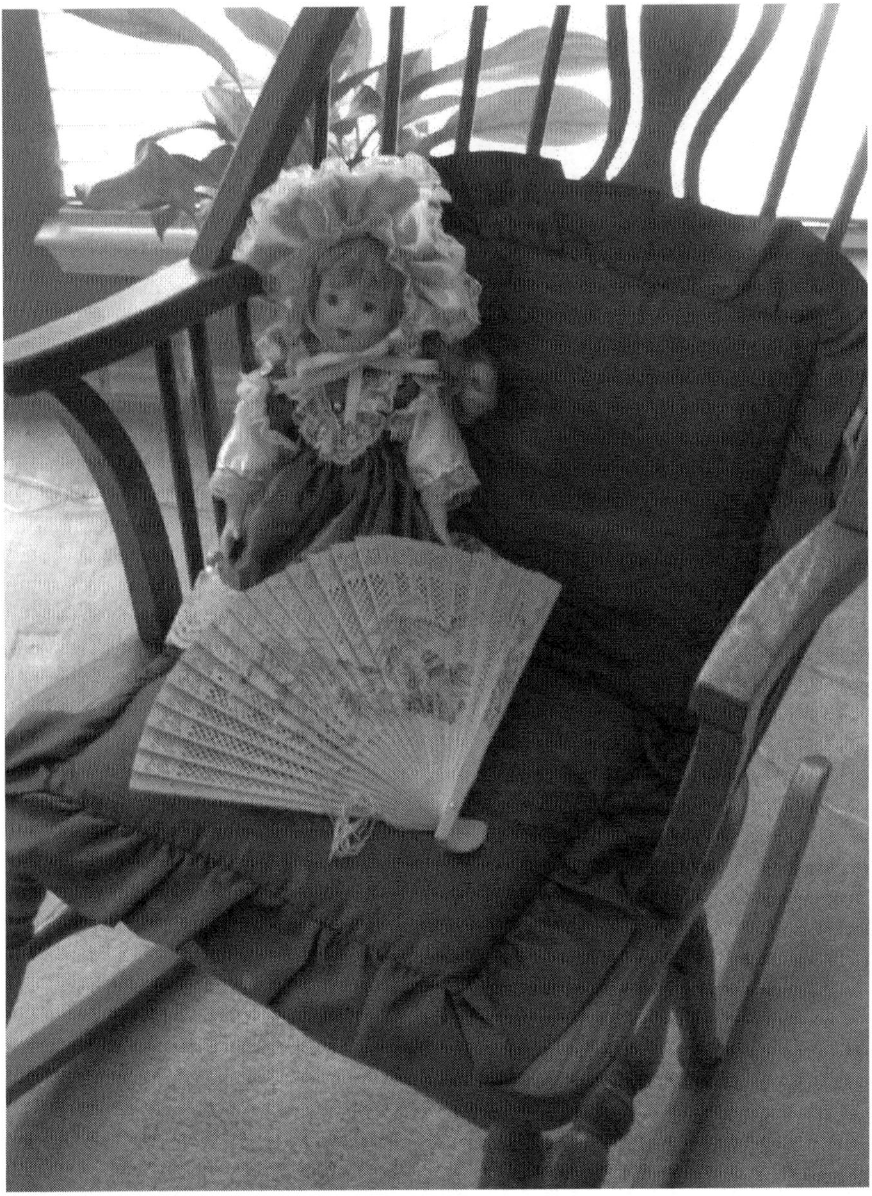

Rocking Chair Wings

When I was very young
and so very very small,
when the world was monstrous and huge
and the night filled with ancient dread
fearful memories and shadows deep,
you were there.
I half remember still the lullabies
of mockingbird gifts, cradles that fall,
hammering and rowing and hands
holding onto the world,
but mostly there is a voice
gentle and soothing and unafraid.
There is a rocking chair,
I am being scolded but I don't care,
I'm in your arms.
When I was still so small
and all is wondrous and new,
I remember being lifted high.
A dancer, a storyteller, a scout,
a poet with a gift for words,
a shy little girl led into her own light.
Before I set my course to sail my sea,
before I climbed to Europe and beyond,
I learned to fly within your arms.
I remember being small, once upon a time.
I can still see the world
wondrous and huge, monstrous and grand,
and I can still feel your hands
and listen to your voice.
No matter how high or far I fly
I remember
it is you who built my wings
and gave me flight.

Strangers

    The buses are closed because of the ice
    and the taxi drivers
    do not know about the train
    to the Great Wall.
    "No train, no train,"
    they say, "Train is full.
    Ride in taxi,
    we take you, we take you,
    two people, two hundred Yuan."

    I am alone, and my guidebook says
    ride the bus.
    It doesn't say
    ride the train.

    "There is a train,"
    says Bali Woman
        to a growing crowd of misplaced tourists,

"There is a train."

We follow Bali Woman,
six in all:
Chinese Couple, though not from Beijing,
Yellow Backpack and Red Coat from Norway,
and Bali Woman and me.

Chinese Couple buy the tickets for the train.
We give them money.
We have an hour to wait;
I buy peanuts.

The train comes.

Red Coat and Yellow Backpack talk about the snow.
"In Norway," they say, "The snow is much higher;
a car left out for the night
could be gone by the morning."
The snow in Beijing is not high,
but it is bitter cold.

We arrive, and the Great Wall is colder still,
cold enough to turn my water bottle
to ice.

We climb up onto the great wall,
stand upon ancient stones,
and look out over China,
walking a path that feet have walked
millennia before.

Afterwards,
together we go to the train,
and back again to where we started.

It is only when we part ways that I realize
I never learned their names.

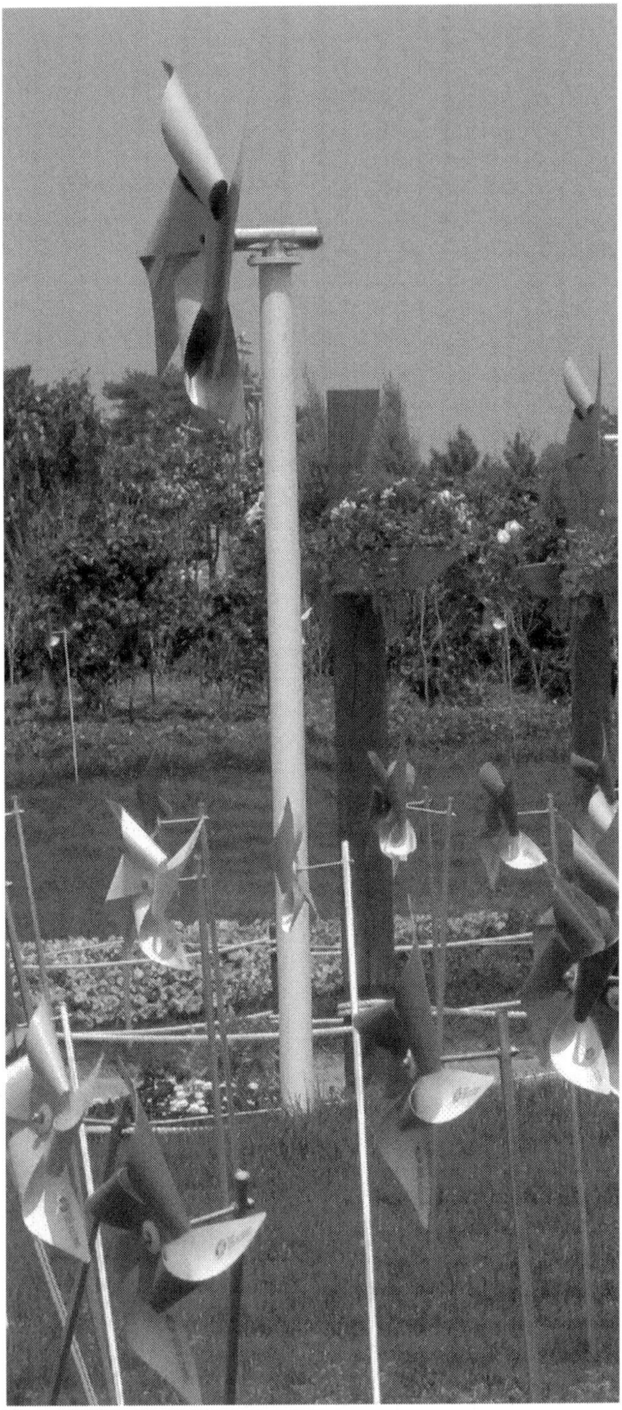

Dance Against the Wind

Tumble little leaf before the mighty wind;
you're lost and alone and there's no one to defend;
tremble yellow, blush red, or fade solemnly to brown;
your sire is bald and has cast away his crown.

The wind hushes like a broom and throws you to the air;
he howls and he sobs and he breaks without a care;
you are cold, little leaf, and you haven't a chance;
you are withered, you are tattered and torn-
      but you dance?

You cannot win, you are already hushed;
fall to the earth to feast upon dust;
you are dead, you are gone, but a ghost of the spring,
a corpse, a memory-
      and yet still you take wing!

Dare you play with the wind? He is larger than you!
He has leveled mountains; what did you ever do?
You can't go but where he throws you like a child with a toy;
you are small, you are helpless, you have no power to destroy.

Go where you are cast; why do you fight,
dance against the wind with no hope in sight?
Tumble little leaf, like a wave upon the sea,
tomorrow you must fall though today you are free.

Why do you play like a kite with the sky?
You are already gone so why do you still try?
The wind was here before you and your grave he will sweep;
your journey should be over, but look how high you leap!

Don't you see it's the end? The world's heavy with snow;
the leveler of stone will never cease to blow;
whole trees are uprooted and bowing blades bend-
        but still you dance,
              and you fall,
                      and you dance against the wind.

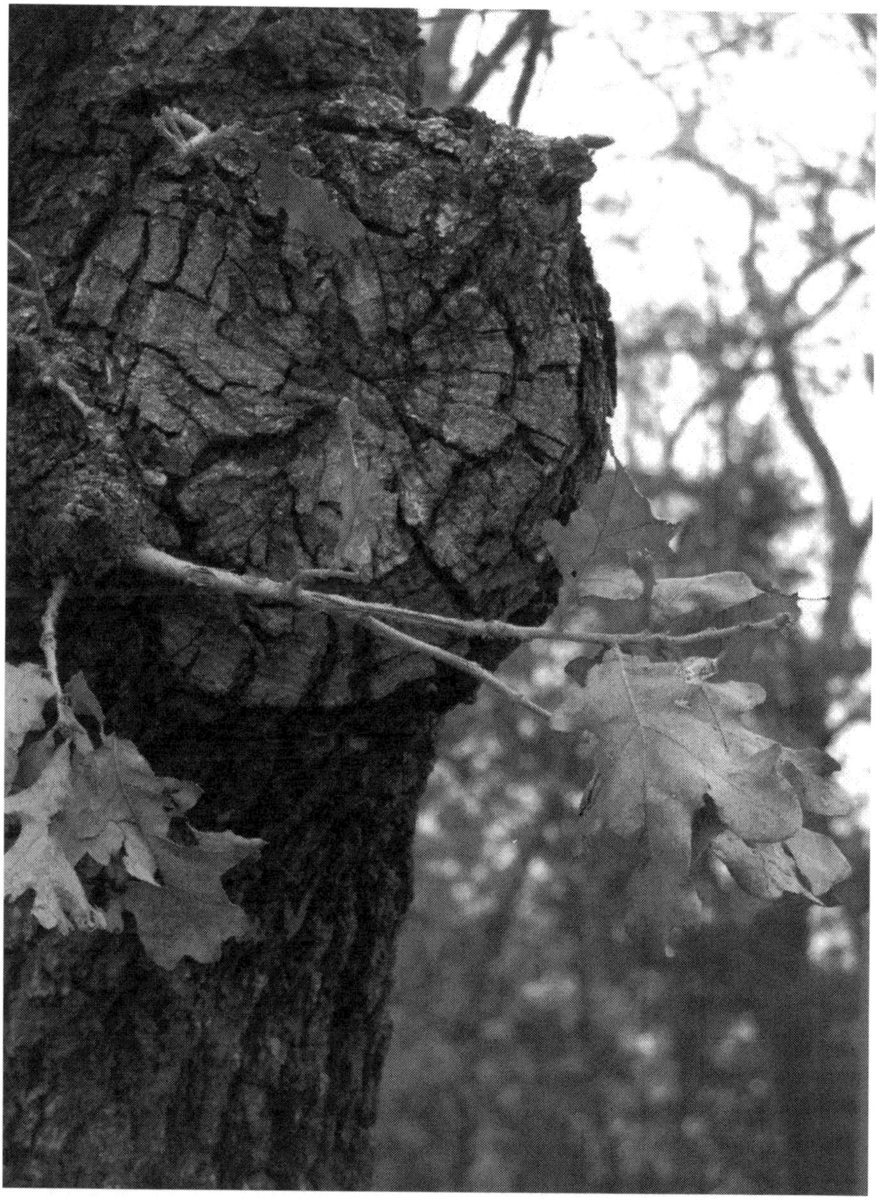

About the Author

Mir Foote has been a writer since the moment she learned to form letters on paper. It is not her career, it is who she is. She has been telling stories since she learned to talk. Stories fueled her childhood play, and poetry soon followed.

She grew up in the country, in a small community called Whitehawk. There she had the woods for her playground, dirt roads for her adventures, and an entire wilderness for inspiration. She was lulled to sleep at night by the sound of drums and coyote calls. By day, she explored.

Now, the world is her playground. She spent a year of school in France and another month in Prague. She taught English for a year in South Korea. She has walked on the Great Wall of China, escaped a forest fire in the mountains of Wyoming, stood in the ruins of Pompeii.

Mir Foote is a world traveler, an amateur linguist, and lover of the written word. She is a teacher. She is a writer. She has published two books to date, and hopes for many more to come.

For more information on her or her books, please go to her website at:

www.mirfoote.com